SOCIAL NETWORKING IS THE NEW COMMUN- ICATION OF THE WORLD

THRU SOCIAL NETWORKS ONE PERSON CAN COMMUNICATE ALL OVER THE WORLD

WITHOUT
HAVING A PASS
PORT. WHEN
SOCIAL
NEWTORKING
STARTED

MYSPACE AND
BLACK PLANET
WAS THE WAY
PEOPLE
COMMUN-
ICATED ACROSS

THE
WORLD.NOW
FACEBOOK
AND TWITTER
IS THE NEW
WAY TO

COMMUNICAT
E WITH
FRIENDS AND
FAMILY. SOCIAL
NETWORK HAS
MADE PLENTY

OF ARTIST
MUCH MONEY.
BECAUSE OF
INTERNET.
ARTIST DO NOT
NEED A

RECORD LABEL
UNLESS IT IS
THEIR CHOICE.
SOLDIER BOY IS
PRIME
EXAMPLE OF

HOW SOCIAL NETWORKING CAN MAKE YOU A WEALTHY PERSON.

SOCIAL

NETWORK GOT
TO A POINT
WHERE PEOPLE
E-THUG. FOR
THOSE THAT
DO NOT KNOW

THE MEANING
OF E-
THUGGING. I
WILL GIVE YOU
A DEFINITION
OF IT WHEN

SOMEONE IS TALKING CRAP. THEY ARE STARTING DRAMA AND OTHER

NEGATIVE.
THRU SOCIAL
NETWORKING
THERE HAVE
BEEN LOT'S OF
DEATHS THAT

COME FROM
SOMEONE
CHATTING
WITH
INDIVIDUALS.
FROM

WORLDSTAR

HIP HOP TO

MEDIA-

TAKEOUT

WHICH IS THE

URBAN SOCIAL

NETWORK
SITES. THESE
WEBSITES ARE
SHOWING THE
WORLD THE
BAD ASPECTS

OF THE URBAN ENVIRON-MENT. TMZ IS ANOTHER POPULAR WEBSITE THAT

SHOWS THE
CELEBRITIES
AND THERE
LIVES. THE
INTERNET IS
THE NEW

MARKET PLACE
FOR IGNORANT
PEOPLE ON ALL
LEVELS. IF
SOMEONE
WANTS GO

VIRAL, ALL
THEY HAVE TO
DO IS ACT
RATCHET
BECAUSE
PEOPLE LOVE

THAT TYPE OF
ENERGY. I
KNOW WHEN
THE INTERNET
BROADCASTS
CHILDREN

THAT ARE
LIVING AN
IMMORAL
LIFESTYLE.
WORLDSTAR
HAS EXPLOITED

THE POOR
PARENTS OF
THE URBAN
ENVIRONMENT
AND ALSO HAS
EXPLOITED

BLACK ON
BLACK CRIME.
THEY ARE
ALWAYS
POSTING BLACK
PEOPLE

FIGHTING EACH OTHER. IN CONCLUSION, USE THE INTERNET TO NETWORK AND

TO BUILD A
BUSINESS THAT
WILL LAST A
LIFETIME.
REMEMBER
THOSE THAT

CREATED THE
SOCIAL
NETWORKS
ARE RICH.

www.ingramcontent.com/pod-product-compliance
Lightning Source LLC
Chambersburg PA
CBHW060938050326
40689CB00013B/3139